Get in the Word
(*for real)

30 Days of
Developing a Relationship with God
Around His Word

Michelle Stimpson
1

Copyright © 2016, Michelle Stimpson
Published by MLStimpson Enterprises, Edify Imprint
P.O. Box 1592
Cedar Hill, TX 75104

ISBN 978-1-943563-07-4

Scripture quotations marked (NIV) are taken from the Holy Bible, New International Version®, NIV®. Copyright © 1973, 1978, 1984, 2011 by Biblica, Inc.™ Used by permission of Zondervan. All rights reserved worldwide. Zondervan.com. The "NIV" and "New International Version" are trademarks registered in the United States Patent and Trademark Office by Biblica, Inc.™

Scripture taken from the Holy Bible, New King James Version (NKJV), ©1979, 1980, 1982 by Thomas Nelson, Inc. Used by permission.

Scripture marked MSG are taken from The Holy Bible, The Message Translation, © 1993, 1994, 1995, 1996, 2000, 2001, 2002 by Eugene H. Peterson. Used by permission.

Scriptures marked KJV taken from the KING JAMES VERSION, public domain.

All rights reserved. No part of this publication may be reproduced, stored in a retrieval system, or transmitted in any form or by any means — electronic, mechanical, photocopy, recording, or any other — except for brief quotations printed in reviews, without the prior permission of the publisher.

Printed in the United States of America
Cover Design by Michelle Stimpson
Edited by Karen McCollum Rodgers

For the Kingdom

Table of Contents

Day 1: Ezekiel 36:12-28
Day 2: 1 John 2:15-17
Day 3: Ephesians 4:28-32
Day 4: Scriptures with Friends - Psalm 119:129-136
Day 5: You Choose the Scripture
Day 6: Philippians 1:15-24
Day 7: John 16:25-33
Day 8: Philippians 3:17-21
Day 9: Scriptures with Friends - Ephesians 1:3-10
Day 10: You Choose the Scripture
Day 11: Isaiah 55:10-11
Day 12: Psalm 147
Day 13: Matthew 9:35-38
Day 14: Scriptures with Friends - Psalm Hebrews 7:23-25
Day 15: You Choose the Scripture
Day 16: Psalm 103
Day 17: 1 Peter 5:6-9
Day 18: 1 John 2:3-6
Day 19: Scriptures with Friends - James 4:7-10
Day 20: You Choose the Scripture
Day 21: Philippians 2:1-13
Day 22: James 2:14-20
Day 23: : Galatians 5:19-22
Day 24: Scriptures with Friends - John 1:6
Day 25: You Choose the Scripture
Day 26: Romans 12:1-2
Day 27: Romans 12:18-21
Day 28: Romans 6:1-14
Day 29: Scriptures with Friends - Haggai 2:1-5
Day 30: You Choose the Scripture
About the Author

Introduction

The purpose of any Christian book is to take you back to the source – the Bible, the inerrant Word of God. This journal-style devotional was created with the same intent. I received the idea for it while discipling a sister in Christ who wanted to use journaling as part of her daily intimate time with the Lord. The problem: She wasn't sure where to start. "What do you do? What are the rules?" she wanted to know. Spontaneously, I handed her one of my journals to read. I didn't even remember what exactly was written in that journal (yikes!). I only knew that sharing it with her would give her a peek into my quiet moments alone with God and, prayerfully, let her see that the holy Scriptures speak to us at our core. She needed to see that believers have Christ living within us—and He *is* the living Word (John 1:1-2). The Bible is who we *be*, not just something we should read or something we should aspire to represent. It's not a checklist—it's our very life. Communing with God around His Word is sweet, fulfilling, and a return to the "cool of the day" fellowship He has always desired with us.

The Scriptures are able to make us wise in our walk. They are also beneficial for teaching, rebuking, correcting, and training us in the righteousness we have in Christ so that we are well-equipped to do what He created us to do (2 Timothy 3:15-16). For this journal, I've included several Scriptures that have impacted me profoundly, but of course there is place for you to explore the Scriptures that have spoken to you. There are also several spots where I've suggested you share your thoughts with a friend. If your friend doesn't already have the book, you can print of those pages so that she can participate using this url: http://bit.ly/GetInTheWord4Real.

Don't limit your prayer life or your quiet time with God to what I have written in these pages. He is infinite! He should in no way be limited to one person's encounters.

Feel free to start with your favorite Scriptures if you see them in the Table of Contents. If you don't see any that are familiar, you can simply go in sequential order—it's really up to you to prayerfully explore these Scriptures as you are led by the Spirit within you.

I use several resources for my side-notes when I study Scripture: biblegateway.com (for various translations); blueletterbible.com (for original Hebrew or Greek words and their literal/non-literal meanings); commentaries (to make sure I understand the context of Scripture), and dictionaries (to refine my understanding of words and search out word origin). All of these resources are available online as well as through phone apps. You can use these, too, as you study the Scriptures on your own.

While these resources are useful tools, I receive the most meaning from the Holy Spirit. He brings other verses to mind, makes connections to the life of Christ in me, relates it to specific circumstances, and informs my prayers.

If you're new to studying the Scriptures, just consider this book "training wheels." I hope you will continue to be taught by Our Father through the Bible long after my marginal snippets of input have ceased. If you have been studying the Word for a while, I hope you'll be able to view the Scriptures with fresh eyes. No matter where you are in your walk, I pray, even now, that God will press these Scriptures (and more) onto your heart as you joyously dig into His Word and know His heart better.

Be blessed,

Michelle Stimpson

Enjoying Our Father with This Book

- Prayerfully read the passage indicated.
- Paraphrase the entire passage. This will help you spot confusion and point you toward seeking clarity. It will also help to internalize the meaning of Scripture.
- On the next page, write down the Scriptures or portions of Scripture that spoke to you.
- "Unpack" the Scripture(s) or portion of Scripture(s) that stuck with you most by asking questions, making notes, commenting, noting definitions, relating to other Scriptures, etc. Feel free to use arrows, drawings, highlighting, etc. to unpack the Scripture.
- Journal – Talk to God (pray in writing) about the Scripture(s) or anything else that the Word brought to mind. It's okay to ask questions, express thanks and even frustrations in your journal — there are no rules! You don't have to fill up all the space. You can staple another piece of paper into the book if you need to. You can record the things you hear Him whispering into your heart. Just be open before God and use this time to get to know Him as Abba, Father.
- Turn the page and view my notes about Scripture(s) from that same passage and how the passage impacted me as well. Please don't think of my thoughts or the excerpts that spoke to me as "the right answers." Just think of my words as an attempt to study and receive Scripture right alongside you. The Holy Spirit is so sensitive and personal that there are things I couldn't include in this book. He has specific things to say to YOU, too! Enjoy this time with Him! This is one of the advantages we have as a believer.

- You will note that there are sections marked "Scriptures with Friends." Follow the same process as before, only this time, share excerpts and study alongside your friends using the printable pages at http://bit.ly/GetInTheWord4Real. Share what you can to edify one another.
- For "You Choose the Scripture" sections, do just that! You might choose to explore Scriptures that have always stumped you, or go even deeper into passages that were mentioned in a sermon. It's up to you. Enjoy!
- Feel free to share your thoughts through social media using the hashtag #GetInTheWord4Real.

Day 1
PRAYERFULLY READ

Ezekiel 36:16-38

Paraphrase: _____

Unpack the Scripture(s) or portions that stuck with you:

Journal

Michelle's paraphrase: *God did this for His name's sake, not the chosen people at that time or for me at this time. He removes filth and idols (v. 25), He gives me a new heart—soft (better to love). CAUSES me to do what pleases Him. Statutes and judgments aren't rules, they are life and love.*

Michelle unpacks the portion that stuck with her:

... I will take the heart of stone out
— This sounds violent. Maybe it needs to be violent
— Stone! Sounds evil. Was my evil? Yes - Jer. 17:19

of your flesh and give you a heart of flesh. I will put My Spirit within you
— cause and effect
→ ordinance

and cause you to walk in My statutes,
↳ cause = fashion, accomplish, make

and you will keep My judgments, and do them.
— observe, give heed
↳ righteous, proper, fitting rule

Ezekiel 36:26-27
NKJV

Michelle's Journal

Abba, Father,

Wow. In a bad way and a good way. Wow in a bad way: The natural state of my heart is "filthy." I never saw it that way, but in light of your holiness, apparently it was. Looking back, I was sometimes afraid to deal with some people because I was afraid I would take advantage of them. And I'll never forget that time I felt this "sneaky" feeling come over me and I gave that boy Nicole's phone number when she didn't even like him. Yes, that was way back in high school, but the point is: I've felt it, the filthy heart. The part of my heart that got jealous and acted ugly when I thought someone was taking advantage of me.

The problem, I see, was in thinking that because I was a "moral" person, I was not exactly filthy. Dirty or dusty or cluttered maybe, but not filthy. THIS is the blindness, the darkness of living a "Christian lifestyle" without knowing You. The deception of "cultural Christianity."

Wow in a good way: Thank You for revealing Yourself to me and saving me!!! YOU clean my heart, YOU put Your Spirit in me and cause me to walk right, talk right, do right.

What, exactly, did I do? Surrender, I guess, but even that I'm not so sure about because the truth is: YOU chose ME, not the other way around. That's how it goes with adoption. I can't do anything but thank You.

Abba, this makes me feel kind of useless. What am I supposed to **DO**?

(Pride and self-sufficiency speaking. I know, God. I know.)

I hear Your whisper: Just BE. Simply BE and believe what I say is so.

I agree. Thank You.

Day 2
PRAYERFULLY READ

1 John 2:15-17

Paraphrase: _____

_____

_____

_____

_____

_____

_____

_____

_____

_____

Unpack the Scripture(s) or portions that stuck with you:

Journal

Michelle's paraphrase: *We can't love the things of the world and love God simultaneously. It's impossible. There's no way to "split" our love. Lust and pride do not come from God but from the world.*

Michelle unpacks the portion that stuck with her:

Do not love the world, or the things of this world. If anyone loves the world, the love of the Father is not in him.   1 John 2:15 NKJV

→ the entirety of earthly goods, riches, advantages that draw us from God

not → does not exist ☹

→ Don't think of the "world" as a globe; it's the kingdom of darkness.

Michelle's Journal

Abba, Father,

This verse really shook me up. I've grown up in a western country. Things of the world are what we are TAUGHT to desire. We go to school to get good jobs so we can have nice things, be admired, live a comfortable lifestyle.

So if I say, "Okay, I'm no longer going to make it my goal to please my flesh with food, have beautiful nice, things that are pleasing to my eye, or to be admired and feel proud of myself," that means I basically am saying, "I'm giving up the American dream," and I don't really know how to replace that dream! What else do I "hope" for and look forward to? If not the big house or the next degree or a more productive business or another piece of red velvet cake, then what? Just live for whatever You make happen? That sounds boring. Pointless. Like I'm not in control. Bingo.

I really don't think I can do what You've called me to do without abandoning all my earthly desires first. This hits me hard with ministry. Maybe some people can balance the two, but there's something in me that hates to mix "business" with "ministry." I know it costs money to print books and fly to conferences and host events. I get that. But I have a hard time keeping my heart pure when I start to put a price on the words You so freely give me to speak. Especially considering all the people who poured into me when I didn't even have the good sense to realize that what they were giving me for free was worth far more than the $10 I was willing to spend on worldly magazines and books every week.

I don't know what I'm supposed to do, but I know it starts here. In Your Word. #surrender.

Day 3
PRAYERFULLY READ

Ephesians 4:28-32

Paraphrase: _____

_____
_____
_____
_____
_____
_____
_____
_____
_____
_____

Unpack the Scripture(s) or portions that stuck with you:

Journal

Michelle's paraphrase: *We must all work to give something to others, use our mouths ONLY to prophecy and edify one another—doing otherwise grieves the Holy Spirit of God. All arguing and bitterness be gone. Love and forgive people the same way God loves and forgives us.*

Michelle unpacks the portion that stuck with her:

→ Surrender part

Let all bitterness, - wickedness, hate
    wrath, - passionate, vengeful anger
    anger, - angry temper
    clamor, - wailing/crying out of distress
and all evil speaking, - speech that injures reputation, slander
    be, - passive (let God do it!)
    put away, - removed, carried away
    from, - separate
    you, - me!
with all malice, - ill-will, desire to injure

    * See James 1:21   Ephesians 4:31
                                        NKJV

Michelle's Journal

Abba, Father,

    I think it's interesting that there is an assumption that these things are in me. That they are inborn. But You would know better than anyone else since You created me. So I must agree with you.

    But our words, God, when they are bad, when they don't build, when they tear people down...it grieves you. I know it's bad for the other person, but the idea that it makes YOU sad is overwhelming.

    This part about "no corrupt word" also hit me hard. The 4th definition of corrupt in Webster: to alter from the original or correct form or version. I suppose in order to not corrupt people with our words, we have to keep at the forefront of our minds the vision YOU have of that person You created because whatever You say is correct.

    I think that when we corrupt other people (as in speak against Your vision of them), it's really a reflection of the corruption within us. Bitterness is a reflection of our resentment/feeling neglected. Anger shows our fear. Distress = feeling alone and without help or remedy. Slander = hate (murderous thoughts). It all comes from sin and reflects a heart that has not found its rest in Your love.

    Father, please do put these things far away from me. Far, far away, so I can stop hurting other people and (most of all) cease to grieve You.

Day 4
SCRIPTURES WITH FRIENDS

Proverbs 4:1-9

Paraphrase: _____

_____
_____
_____
_____
_____
_____
_____
_____
_____
_____

Unpack the Scripture(s) or portions that stuck with you:

Journal

Day 5
YOU CHOOSE THE SCRIPTURE

Scripture(s): _____

Paraphrase: _____
_____
_____
_____
_____
_____
_____
_____
_____
_____
_____
_____

Unpack the Scripture(s) or portions that stuck with you:

Journal

Day 6
Prayerfully Read

Philippians 1:15-24

Paraphrase: _____

_____

_____

_____

_____

_____

_____

_____

_____

_____

_____

Unpack the Scripture(s) or portions that stuck with you:

Journal

Michelle's paraphrase: *Some people were preaching the gospel because it was gaining popularity and gave them a platform to become well-known (selfish ambitions). Others were spreading the gospel from a pure heart. Paul said it didn't matter what a person's ambitions were—so long as the gospel was preached; that's what mattered. Furthermore, he wasn't completely excited about the idea of sticking around on Earth because being here meant being separated from Christ, in the flesh (which is not desirable). But Paul chose to stay because it would help others.*

Michelle unpacks the portion that stuck with her:

For me, to live is Christ [the Messiah], and to die is gain [advantage].
↳ Paul (believer-apostle, not everyone)

Philippians 1:21
NKJV

Michelle's Journal

Abba, Father,

First of all, God, Paul's perspective is so refreshing to me. Thank You for the Scriptures!

I agree with Paul. This life (living in skin, always having to be on guard, always discipling and giving to other people who aren't always appreciative, pouring out ourselves even to the point of persecution) is NOT desirable. It's noble. It's beautiful. And I mean, it's not terrible. You said You would never leave us. We have Your Spirit within us, and we do have victory in Christ.

But these battles we fight—they are time-consuming. And if given the choice between living on Earth and going with You, I don't know that I'm patient enough to choose living here. Sometimes I do wish our bodies could just drop dead right at salvation and return home to You. This world is so JACKED! I'm so glad it's not my home. I'd be completely hopeless without the promise of an eternity with You. I would probably bury myself with work and then go home every day and self-medicate my fears and anxieties with candy and count down the days until...what? Nothingness?

Oh. My. You. What a depressing thought.

Back to reality. The point of living this life is Christ. Period. Dying is not the worst thing that happens to a believer. Quite the opposite. It's one of the BEST things that will ever happen to us! It is gain!

Day 7
PRAYERFULLY READ

John 16:25-33

Paraphrase: _____

Unpack the Scripture(s) or portions that stuck with you:

Journal

Michelle's paraphrase: *Jesus speaks clearly to the disciples (not in figurative language) because they are ready to hear Him now that they believe He is sent from the Father. He tells them more, and in clear language, so that they will not be afraid. Jesus knows there will be trouble, but He doesn't want them to be afraid of the trouble because He has overcome the trouble.*

Michelle unpacks the portion that stuck with her:

... In the world, ye shall have tribulation,

- world → earth, place inhabited by men, ruled by prince of darkness (but the isn't the king!)
- tribulation → pressing, pressure, affliction (2 Cor 4:8-10)

but be of good cheer; I have overcome, the
↳ emerged with victory

world.

John 16:33
KJV

Michelle's Journal

Abba, Father,

Ooooh wee! This is so poignant for me right now as I make the transition from writing fiction to non-fiction. I like writing novels, creating characters, creating plots and teaching lessons through those plots. But there is also a time to speak directly to my brothers and sisters. Thank You for this today! And thank you for the conversation with Rhonda McKnight. It's interesting to me that You are moving several of us fiction folks into non-fiction. The Movement is On! I'm not going to fight it anymore. I surrender!

Now, there will be trouble. Wait—there was always trouble!!! We should not even hope that there will be no trouble. The difference in our lives is this Word, this promise from Jesus that the tribulation (the pressure) can't overtake us because He has overcome it.

I remember when I was at the hospital about to give birth to Kalen and I had the epidural. They told me that I would feel pressure, but not pain. And they were right. I knew something was happening, I could feel and see my body going through motions. It wasn't necessarily comfortable, but I was numb to the brunt of it because of the block.

I think this is probably a bad analogy, but in some ways, Jesus is the block. He's the One who stands in our stead and bears the brunt of the world's brutality. He softens blows, reduces pain to pressure, changes our perception of what's going on around us even though it _is_ still happening.

Father, help me to see the tribulation for what it is: An opportunity to get a Jesus eye-view in life.

Day 8
PRAYERFULLY READ

Philippians 3:17-21

Paraphrase: _____

_____

_____

_____

_____

_____

_____

_____

_____

_____

_____

Unpack the Scripture(s) or portions that stuck with you:

Journal

Michelle's paraphrase: *Paul tells them to follow the example of godliness has been set. There are many people living as enemies of the Cross. They have destructive lifestyles and they're proud of it. They and live for glory in this world. That's not who believers are. We are not even citizens here, and one day our heavenly bodies will show it!*

Michelle unpacks the portion that stuck with her:

But our ⌞citizenship⌝ is in ⌞heaven⌟... → not America, not even earth

↓
Kingdom to whom we claim allegiance; part of a sense of identity, I think

Philippians 3:20
NIV

Michelle's Journal

Abba, Father,

It's so hard not to become entangled in the affairs of this world sometimes. When I see injustice in America or anywhere in the world, I want to just run out and march down the streets turning cartwheels and screaming, "Stop the madness!"

There are so many worthy causes—poor, starving, sick, trafficked, abused and persecuted people. Not to mention the harm we bring to animals and the environment. I know You want us to help people and relieve suffering as much as we can.

But this is the way of the world. You gave us the book of Revelation. We know how this is going to turn out. We know that this world is passing away. It's getting darker with every generation. And yet, believers have never had more of an opportunity than now to be a light. People need You! People need Jesus! People need the assurance of Your indwelling Holy Spirit during these times!

This is the team I am on. Like the angel (in Joshua 5:13-14), I must remember that I'm not here simply to represent women, African-Americans, Americans, a political party, a state, or a stance on educational policy. I'm here to represent the Kingdom.

I'm not here to take sides—I'm here to take over.

Day 9
SCRIPTURES WITH FRIENDS

Ephesians 1:3-10

Paraphrase: _____

_____

_____

_____

_____

_____

_____

_____

_____

_____

_____

Unpack the Scripture(s) or portions that stuck with you:

Journal

Day 10
You Choose the Scripture

Scripture(s): _____

Paraphrase: _____
_____
_____
_____
_____
_____
_____
_____
_____
_____
_____
_____

Unpack the Scripture(s) or portions that stuck with you:

Journal

Day 11
PRAYERFULLY READ

Isaiah 55:10-11

Paraphrase: _____

Unpack the Scripture(s) or portions that stuck with you:

Journal

Michelle's paraphrase: *Just like rain and snow come down from heaven and water the earth and make the ground produce flowers and such, so does God's Word come from His mouth to the earth and do what it does. Whatever He sends the Word to do, it does.*

Michelle unpacks the portion that stuck with her:

So <u>shall</u> my <u>word</u> be that goeth forth out of my mouth: it shall not return unto me <u>void</u>, but <u>it</u> shall <u>accomplish</u> that which I <u>please</u>, and it shall <u>prosper</u> in the thing whereto I sent it.

→ not "might", not "I hope so"
→ see Psalm 138:2
→ His word!
→ do work, make
↳ with no effect
↳ delight, desire
↳ succeed, make progress

Isaiah 55:11
KJV

Michelle's Journal

Abba, Father,

    I love this Scripture, God, because it reminds me of that time You went off on Job and his friends for conjecturing all this foolishness. You came in like: Y'all must not know who you're dealing with. Dudes, lightning bolts come and ask me where to go! (Job 38:35) I'm always amazed by that Scripture, Lord, because I just see a bunch of these huge, thunderous bolts scooting over to You and bowing down, waiting for Your directions. You are All That!!!

    Verse 11 says the same happens with all precipitation—You assign it work, and it does the work. Not once has a drop of rain come back to You and said, "I'm sorry, God, but I couldn't do what You told me to do because there was this big car in the way." Um...no! Water finds its way to the Earth and does what it has to do. Every time. Even if someone collected the water and used it for making spaghetti, that water would find its way into a stream, then up into a cloud, drifting 100 miles away, and then to a plant somewhere that was thirsty.

    Your Word is the same. It doesn't come back not having done what You sent it to do. No one can stop it. No one can keep it from manifesting. That's the thing about You, God—Your ultimate purpose always prevails. I don't think You "control" everything, but You are sovereign. Even when people are disobedient, even when evil is present, even when things get delayed or re-routed, Your will still prevails. That's what makes You God.

    There's nobody like You.

Day 12
PRAYERFULLY READ

Psalm 147

Paraphrase: _____

_____
_____
_____
_____
_____
_____
_____
_____
_____

Unpack the Scripture(s) or portions that stuck with you:

Journal

Michelle's paraphrase: *God is so good. So powerful. He is infinite. He doesn't need the strength of horses or people—He only delights in our reverence and trust. He guards, He blesses, He runs the Earth, even down to the details. His children have the advantage.*

Michelle unpacks the portion that stuck with her:

The LORD takes <u>pleasure</u> [→ delight ☺], in those who <u>fear</u> [→ reverent fear], Him, In those who hope in <u>His mercy</u> [→ not in ourselves or our goodness].

Psalm 147: 11
NKJV

Michelle's Journal

Abba, Father,

I've been thinking a lot about what You really like. Kind of like how I buy Christmas gifts. I want to know what that other person wants, what would make them smile when they open that gift.

(By the way, God, it really irks me when people say that we need to do good so we'll have all these brownie-point rewards in heaven. How self-serving is that? And aren't we earning crowns so we can cast them at Your feet anyway?)

I see in this Scripture that You want our reverence—a holy respect for You. You want us to recognize Who we're dealing with! I admit: For as much as I know You and talk to You and am familiar with You, I don't think I fully realize what it means to have the ear of the One who created everything. It's too big for my brain. I still want more reverence anyway.

You also want my trust. My hope. Wow—that feels scary to me. If I give you all my hopes and dreams (like that William McDowell song, "I Give Myself Away"), what will You do with them? You are good and You will be glorified in the end. I guess I just want to know beforehand.

But that wouldn't be trust then, would it? It would probably be Michelle trying to figure out a way to make the process as painless as possible. To save a little piece of me for me.

But You want all of me. And I want this gift for You. I pray that Your Spirit gives You what You want in me. Be it unto me according to Your Word.

Day 13
PRAYERFULLY READ

Matthew 9:35-38

Paraphrase: _____

_____
_____
_____
_____
_____
_____
_____
_____
_____
_____

Unpack the Scripture(s) or portions that stuck with you:

Journal

Michelle's paraphrase: *Jesus went to many cities and villages teaching, preaching, and healing. But he was overwhelmed with compassion for the people who were so lost. He told the disciples that there were plenty of people who needed help, but few available to do the work of harvesting these scattered souls. He said they should pray for harvesters.*

Michelle unpacks the portion that stuck with her:

But when He [Jesus] saw the multitudes,

→ His heart for people ♥

He was moved with <u>compassion,</u> for them,

→ weak, harrassed

because they were <u>weary,</u> and scattered, like

<u>sheep having no shepherd.</u>

↳ what happens to sheep without a shepherd? Can they survive in the wild on their own?

Matthew 9:36
NKJV

Michelle's Journal

Abba, Father,

Verse 36 really hit me because Christ's reaction to weak people is to have compassion. Not disgust. Not tough love. Not a shaking of the head.

No. Compassion.

I think I've had my mind tainted by my culture. We pride ourselves on pulling ourselves up by the bootstraps and on the idea that those who are weak somehow deserve their condition. Social Darwinism. A spirit of competition. The weak should "man up," be stronger. Not be such whiney babies. After all, this is America. The land of opportunity. Build a bridge and get over yourself.

First off: the word weak also means "harassed." As in: Somebody is messing with them. We know who that somebody is.

Second: Blaming my "culture" is the easy way out. This tendency to stomp on the weak rather than feel their pain, pray for their relief, and/or offer help is a tell-tale sign of pride.

God, You know how I feel when I'm around whiney, needy people. I feel indignant. But the real problem is that I feel the same way about myself when I feel weak.

Yet, weakness, brokenness is what you require.

I repent. I receive the heart of Christ for the weak. I identify myself as "the weak" with regard to You. I want You to lead me like the meek, humble sheep You've called me because, in truth, that's exactly what I BE.

Day 14
SCRIPTURES WITH FRIENDS

Hebrews 7:23-25

Paraphrase: _____

Unpack the Scripture(s) or portions that stuck with you:

Journal

Day 15
YOU CHOOSE THE SCRIPTURE

Scripture(s): _____

Paraphrase: _____
_____
_____
_____
_____
_____
_____
_____
_____
_____
_____
_____

Unpack the Scripture(s) or portions that stuck with you:

Journal

Day 16
PRAYERFULLY READ

Psalm 103:1-14

Paraphrase: _____

Unpack the Scripture(s) or portions that stuck with you:

Journal

Michelle's paraphrase: *God's people have great benefits in Him. He acts on our behalf, He is gracious and merciful toward us, and He pities us because He knows how frail and weak we actually are.*

Michelle unpacks the portion that stuck with her:

The LORD is merciful and gracious, → pleasantly kind (see His ♥ and humility!)

Slow to anger and abounding in mercy.

Psalm 103:8
NKJV

Michelle's Journal

Abba, Father,

    I feel like weeping right now at Your goodness. It's overwhelming. YOU are overwhelming, God. It would be enough that we have an eternity with You, but You decided to start our eternity NOW by giving us Your Spirit (which is even more than the Old Testament believer who wrote this Psalm had). You forgive, heal, redeem, crown, satisfy, and renew us. That's a lot of stuff, Lord, and we don't even deserve it. Your heart is beautiful.

    You make Yourself and Your ways known to us. You put our sins as far as the east is from the west. You do all this out of Your kindness and humility!

    God, You must really feel sorry for us. I'm looking at Verses 13-14 again. You "pity" us. I'm sure we are a pitiful group of sheep (baaa! baaaa!). Were it not for You, we would follow each other off of cliffs and into deep, treacherous waters to drown.

    I love that You have given us this illustration of Your love toward us as father toward His children. I remember the day I busted out the back window of my dad's 1956 Chevrolet with a rock. I was terrified, but he never punished me. He said he wasn't angry because he knew it was an accident.

    Well, You know how frail and vulnerable we are. You correct us when our acts aren't accidents, but even in that You are merciful. It's never as bad as it could have been because no matter what, we still have eternity with You.

    This is the love You have for us and I, for one, am grateful!

Day 17
PRAYERFULLY READ

1 Peter 5:6-9

Paraphrase: _____

Unpack the Scripture(s) or portions that stuck with you:

Journal

Michelle's paraphrase: *Be humble before God. Let Him exalt you in due time. Let Him bear the weight of our troubles and concerns. And watch out for the enemy's attacks. He is always trying to bully believers into surrendering our power to him. Resist him, as so many others all over the world are already doing.*

Michelle unpacks the portion that stuck with her:

Be self-controlled, and alert. Your enemy the devil prowls around like a roaring lion, looking for someone to devour. Resist him, standing firm in the faith.

- self-controlled → Sober
- alert → watching (not actively passive)
- roaring lion → But lions don't roar when they actually look for prey???
- devour → swallow, drink
- Resist → actively oppose

1 Peter 5:8, 9a
(Translation?)

Michelle's Journal

Abba, Father,

That word "sober" speaks a lot. Sober = have a clear mind that's not under the influence of some substance (my definition).

In fact, I just had a talk with someone about how he believes that drinking alcohol makes him a better dancer at the club. I seriously doubt that he had better moves after a few drinks (especially considering the fact that he can't dance anyway, period). But an un-sober mind doesn't process things as they are.

The believer who is not sober sees the enemy like a roaring lion. First off, lions don't roar when they are on the prowl—that would give them away. A lion would never get to eat gazelle if he rolled up with a roar. That's the thing about our adversary, though, he knows he cannot devour us. Christ already swallowed <u>him</u> up in victory. Christ lives in us, so the enemy can't swallow the One who has already swallowed him! All he can do is try to scare us. Thus the roar. It's an attempt to put fear into us and cause us to run around like the sky is falling, like we don't know You're holding up the sky in the first place.

Resist, You say. Tell him to shut-up. And I love this last part: People (our brothers and sisters in Christ all over the world) have already gone down this path. Even those who were martyred for the faith rose again in victory with Christ. We always win. Always. The enemy knows this. And You, Father, want us to know this, too.

Day 18
PRAYERFULLY READ

1 John 2:3-6

Paraphrase: _____

Unpack the Scripture(s) or portions that stuck with you:

Journal

Michelle's paraphrase: *Those who know God keep His commandments. Whoever says he knows God but does not keep His commandments is lying. But whoever keeps God's Word is perfected in God's love. There ought to be a correlation between our walk in Christ and our lifestyles.*

Michelle unpacks the portion that stuck with her:

But whoever ⎣Keeps⎦ His word, truly the love of God is ⎣perfected⎦ in Him. By this we know that we are in Him.   1 John 2:5 NKJV

↗ attend carefully, guard, observe

↘ perfect, complete, accomplished, finished (John 19:30)

↗ (James 1:4)

Abba, Father,

    Just this morning I was asking You a lot of questions about salvation and the church:

1) Are there people who truly believe they are going to heaven because they repeated the "prayer of faith" when, in actuality, they are not saved?

2) Is the absence of a thirst for Your commandments/Your Word a clear indication that a person really doesn't know You?

3) If a person does not "know" You, does that mean he or she did not believe on Christ as the payment for their sin? Can't a person believe but not ever truly get to know You (like the thief at the cross)?

4) Do I even need to concern myself with this? Is this a mystery beyond my understanding that I need to let go and just trust that You know people's hearts and You will figure it out (separate wheat from tares) later?

    God, I do not know exactly what's going on with us Christians. I get a sense that there are a lot of rule-followers (Type-As) who like the idea that the good guys win in the end, thus Christianity fits their personality), but they are not necessarily Christ-followers. They are moral, but not actually believers.

    Only You can know the heart of a man and judge accordingly. I just feel sad because I don't want people to live their lives with a false sense of eternal security. This concerns me.

    But I surrender my right to know it all. I trust that You know Your sheep and Your sheep know Your voice and obey (John 10:27). Thank You.

Day 19
SCRIPTURES WITH FRIENDS

James 4:7-10

Paraphrase: _____

Unpack the Scripture(s) or portions that stuck with you:

Journal

Day 20
YOU CHOOSE THE SCRIPTURE

Scripture(s): _____

Paraphrase: _____
_____
_____
_____
_____
_____
_____
_____
_____
_____
_____

Unpack the Scripture(s) or portions that stuck with you:

Journal

Day 21
PRAYERFULLY READ

Philippians 2:1-13

Paraphrase: _____

Unpack the Scripture(s) or portions that stuck with you:

Journal

Michelle's paraphrase: *Believers must love one another from the source of our common love. Be as humble as Christ, who was God in the flesh, but lowered Himself to be a human. Keep doing what God would have us to do even when no one is looking. Truly, God works in us to think and act like Christ.*

Michelle unpacks the portion that stuck with her:

... work out your own salvation with fear and trembling; for it is God who works, in you both
↳ energeo (present, active)

to ①will and to ②do for His good pleasure.
  ↳have   ↳action,
  in mind   working, put
             forth power

Philippians 2:12-13
NKJV

Michelle's Journal

Abba, Father,

I LOVE these Scriptures! Your heart is so clear. You never asked us to do it all. You didn't even say You would "help us" do it all. You said You would work IN US!

Verse 13 has especially changed my thoughts. I heard You when You told me never to say/pray again, "God, I need Your help…" because to say that I "need" something is to imply that I lack something, and I will never lack You because You promised to never leave or forsake me. Rather, I'm confessing, "God, I thank You that I have You today as I…"

The second thing: Don't ever say "God, I have a lot to do today." My new statement, "God, You are doing a lot in me today."

At first I thought You were really just fussing, but I know You, Father. You are so purposeful. It's these little phrases, these tiny prepositions, these small foxes that program our minds to either: 1) believe that You are doing Your work IN us (Ezekiel 36:26-27); or 2) believe that we are relying on ourselves primarily with a little help from You once we have done all we can do (my part, God's part philosophy).

Thank You for the promise of Your Holy Spirit to do this in us. Your plan is brilliant!!! Your ways are the BEST!!!

Day 22
PRAYERFULLY READ

James 2:14-20

Paraphrase: _____

Unpack the Scripture(s) or portions that stuck with you:

Journal

Michelle's paraphrase: *It's one thing to say we have faith, another to show it, to live like it. We don't perform works to prove faith. Our works are the fruit of our faith. If we have no fruit, was there ever a root in the first place?*

Michelle unpacks the portion that stuck with her:

Thus also <u>faith</u>, by itself, if it does not have
  ↳ Give faith something to do!
<u>works</u>, is <u>dead</u>. → can it exist but still be dead?
  ↳ occupation, employment

James 2:17
NKJV

Michelle's Journal

Abba, Father,

OK. Here I am again wrestling with this outward vs. inward theme.

Maybe it's because You made me such an artist. Such an anti-Type-A (am I a Z-type?). I just really love how Jesus did things with the Pharisees—the people who wanted to be right by virtue of the fact they'd kept all those rules. I guess I would be a little upset, too, if my family and I for generations back had spent all of our lives obeying all these ordinances and then somebody came along and said, "Rules have changed. You don't have to do that anymore. Slate's cleared. You're all clear if You believe on The Messiah, even those of you who have never, ever, ever done anything right."

But like you told Jonah, who are we—the creation—to be upset at the mercy of the Creator? You are generously merciful to ALL!

So, yes, Lord, I love Your Word. I love the way You make self-righteous people mad.

And then there's this Scripture which, at first glance, seems to point us toward works as "proof" of our faith.

But the heart question has to be: Who is doing the proving to Whom? Surely it's not us doing the proving to other people. What good would that do? No. It is You proving Yourself in us, proving Your good and perfect will in Your people (Romans 12:2). Thank You for confirming us through and through (1 Thessalonians 5:23-24).

Day 23
PRAYERFULLY READ

Galatians 5:19-22

Paraphrase: _____
_____
_____
_____
_____
_____
_____
_____
_____
_____
_____
_____

Unpack the Scripture(s) or portions that stuck with you:

Journal

Michelle's paraphrase: *Walk in the Spirit and we won't find ourselves subject to the power of the flesh. The things the flesh invokes are evident. So are the things produced by a life lived in obedience to the Spirit.*

Michelle unpacks the portion that stuck with her:

But the <u>fruit of the spirit</u> is... <u>self-control</u>...
              cause ————————→ effect

→ mastery of desires/passions (especially pertaining to sensual)

Galatians 5:22
NKJV

Michelle's Journal

Abba, Father,

Verse 19 is so freeing. I think the enemy tries to convince us that we are worse than the average person when, in reality, all those things listed are simply the fruit of walking under his influence.

This self-control is life! I do wonder if self-control is the same thing as dying "daily?" (1 Corinthians 15:31) If something has to die every day, does that mean it comes back to life every night? Who does that—zombies???

Here's something else: Fruit doesn't last forever. We need new fruit. Fresh fruit just like we need fresh grace and mercy every morning (Lamentations 3:22-23).

So self-control isn't necessarily a once-and-for-all thing. Flesh was overcome at the cross. We rely on Jesus' one-time death, burial, and resurrection fresh every day. (It has to be like that, or else He'd have to die again every so often for a fresh new batch of sinners.) I must remind the flesh who's boss! This is the daily death! Speaking Your Word is the daily funeral!

I see You, Father. You like to renew. You like fresh. You like continuous growth and pruning and rain and cleansing and such. New flowers every year, new generation of people every 20 years, Christ constantly interceding for us (Hebrews 7:25).

I have read these Scriptures before, but this is something You are showing me about Yourself for the first time. I love it!!!

Day 24
SCRIPTURES WITH FRIENDS

2 John 1:6

Paraphrase: _____
_____
_____
_____
_____
_____
_____
_____
_____
_____
_____
_____

Unpack the Scripture(s) or portions that stuck with you:

Journal

Day 25
You Choose the Scripture

Scripture(s): _____

Paraphrase: _____
_____
_____
_____
_____
_____
_____
_____
_____
_____
_____
_____

Unpack the Scripture(s) or portions that stuck with you:

Journal

Day 26
Prayerfully Read

Romans 12:1-2

Paraphrase: _____

_____
_____
_____
_____
_____
_____
_____
_____
_____
_____

Unpack the Scripture(s) or portions that stuck with you:

Journal

Michelle's paraphrase: *Don't adopt your norms from society at large. Reject them completely in order to know God's perfect will and ways.*

Michelle unpacks the portion that stuck with her:

And be not conformed [→ fashion one's self] to this world: but be transformed [↳ change into another form], by the renewing [↓ Complete change for the better] of your mind... [↳ See Eph. 4:23]

Romans 12:1 KJV

Michelle's Journal

Abba, Father,

"Not conformed." Sounds uncivilized, like somebody who doesn't know the social norms. It's probably the quickest way to get kicked out of the "in" crowd.

God, I don't think I've never been out of the "in" crowd until recently. My crowd has always been "church folk" and "good people" but the more I delve into Your Word—particularly the New Testament—the more I see a huge disparity.

But forget about them (for now)—what about me? How much of what I do and think and say is really just borne of the traditions of men? In particular, I've had to revisit a lot of things in recent years: 1) "Scriptures" that aren't even in the Bible; 2) church songs that have no biblical basis; 3) connection to a sorority; 4) church traditions that work against the grace of Christ.

I know we don't need to get caught up in minor disagreements. But if we are going to do what Romans 12:1 says, we must have the discernment to know what is worldly vs. what is Word.

God, when I read this and think about all that You have already changed in me, I'm thinking, "What _else_ am I doing right now that has _nothing_ to do with God's ways?"

But I will not get anxious. I know You will show me. You always do. Thank You!!!

Day 27
PRAYERFULLY READ

Romans 12:18-21

Paraphrase: _____

Unpack the Scripture(s) or portions that stuck with you:

Journal

Michelle's paraphrase: *Do not treat people the way they deserve to be treated. Be gracious. Do your best to get along with people, and do not try to out-do other people's evil with more evil.*

Michelle unpacks the portion that stuck with her:

Do not be ⎣overcome⎦ by evil, but overcome evil with good.

→ Conquered, carried off as spoil — reminds me of a shark dragging its prey to the depths in order to drown it and eat it

Romans 12:21 KJV

Michelle's Journal

Abba, Father,

That vision that popped into my mind of the shark was so clear. Responding to evil with evil is so damning for everyone involved. Descending into total enemy territory.

Show me that picture again, Lord, the next time I decide to "shut down" on my husband in response to him. Show me how I'm throwing myself into the shark's mouth so he can take me some place where I can't even breathe, can't function.

The times when I have "shut down" only led to depressive episodes. It's like not only am I mad at my husband, I stop folding clothes, start eating junk like crazy, stop being productive, get bombarded by all these thoughts about how much better my life would have been if this or that had happened—it's quite suffocating. And I don't know that I've ever realized (until I read this Scripture again today) that the way I got there was by trying to overcome evil with evil. It's more than the idea that two wrongs don't make a right. Two wrongs usher in stealing, killing, and destruction (John 10:10).

But if after one wrong somebody does right, this stuff gets handled on the surface. And You get the glory.

Hallelujah! No more shark take-downs here, thanks to Your Word!

Day 28
Prayerfully Read

Romans 6:1-14

Paraphrase: _____

Unpack the Scripture(s) or portions that stuck with you:

Journal

Michelle's paraphrase: *By His grace, we have dominion over sin. How is it possible to be ruler of something and still live under its power as if Christ never died for us? We have been buried with Him, we rose with Him, and this is our new place in Him. Be alive unto God through Christ. Receive this new life of grace and stop trying to justify yourself through the law.*

Michelle unpacks the portion that stuck with her:

For sin shall not have dominion over you: *[annotation: be lord/ruler of, exercise power/influence]*

for ye are not under the law, but under grace.

[annotation: Was I ever under the law anyway since I am a Gentile?]

Romans 6:14 KJV

Michelle's Journal

Abba, Father,

(I do wonder about that Gentile thing, God. I don't guess it matters now, though, because I am under grace regardless.)

But this first part of Verse 14.

Oh. My. YOU!

It makes me think about the relationship between believers and sin. There is a relationship, after all. The relationship is: authority to subject. We have the authority in Christ to exercise dominion over sin and the one who influences us to sin.

When the enemy came to You about Job (Job 1:6), You were like: What are you doing here? What do you want? Let me tell you what you can and cannot do... Now, bye.

Though evil was present, it was very clear who was the Boss of whom. (You are my hero.)

The very fact that the enemy approached You (and Jesus in Matthew 4:1-11) lets me know that he can also approach me. (Evil present does not make me an evil person.)

I want to be like You and Jesus, Father. I don't want to run and hide and leave my territory abandoned when evil is near. I want to be like: Who's that knocking at my door? Whatchu want? No. I'm not buying it. It is written... Go somewhere else with that foolishness. Bye.

Day 29
SCRIPTURES WITH FRIENDS

Haggai 2:1-5

Paraphrase: _____

_____
_____
_____
_____
_____
_____
_____
_____
_____
_____
_____
_____

Unpack the Scripture(s) or portions that stuck with you:

Journal

Day 30
YOU CHOOSE THE SCRIPTURE

Scripture(s): _____

Paraphrase: _____
_____
_____
_____
_____
_____
_____
_____
_____
_____

Unpack the Scripture(s) or portions that stuck with you:

Journal

About the Author

Michelle Stimpson, founder of Warrior Wives Club, is a national bestselling author, an educator, and a speaker who has trained thousands of women on everything from writing life stories to getting along with spouses. She has benefited greatly from the advice and wisdom of seasoned Christian women and is anointed to work with wives who are facing difficulties in marriage. As such, she is a popular workshop facilitator and always leaves her audiences thirsting for more of God's Word and His ways.

Michelle is a part-time educational consultant with an M.Ed. who uses her gifts and formal training to build the Kingdom for generations to come.

Visit her online at www.MichelleStimpson.com or www.WarriorWives.Club. Connect through social media at:
Facebook.com/MichelleStimpsonWrites
Facebook.com/WarriorWivesClub
@StimpsonWrites (Twitter)

More Books by Michelle Stimpson

Non-Fiction
Did I Marry the Wrong Guy? And other Silent Ponderings of a Fairly Normal Christian Wife
Married for Five Minutes: Hope for Living Inside Real-Life Marriages
Uncommon Sense: 30 Truths to Radically Renew Your Mind in Christ
The 21-Day Publishing Plan
War Room Strategies: Developing Effectual Prayers for God's Glory

Fiction
A Forgotten Love (Book 1 - A Few Good Men)
The Start of a Good Thing (Book 2 - A Few Good Men)
A Change of Heart (Book 3 – A Few Good Men)
Stuck On You (Book 1 - The Stoneworths)
All This Love Book 2 - Stoneworths)
A Shoulda Woulda Christmas
Boaz Brown Book 1 in Boaz Brown Series
No Weapon Formed Book 2 in the Boaz Brown Series
Divas of Damascus Road
Falling into Grace
I Met Him in the Ladies' Room
I Met Him in the Ladies' Room Again
Last Temptation
Mama B: A Time to Speak (Book 1)
Mama B: A Time to Dance (Book 2)
Mama B: A Time to Love (Book 3)
Mama B: A Time to Mend (Book 4)
Mama B: A Time for War (Book 5)
Mama B: A Time to Plant (Book 6)
Someone to Watch Over Me
Stepping Down
The Good Stuff
The Blended Blessings Series (co-authored with CaSandra McLaughlin)
The What About? Series (co-authored with April Barker)
Trouble In My Way

www.ingramcontent.com/pod-product-compliance
Lightning Source LLC
Chambersburg PA
CBHW021439080526
44588CB00009B/603